HISTORY DUDES
ANCIENT EGYPTIANS

ILLUSTRATED BY
RICH CANDO

WRITTEN BY
LAURA BULLER

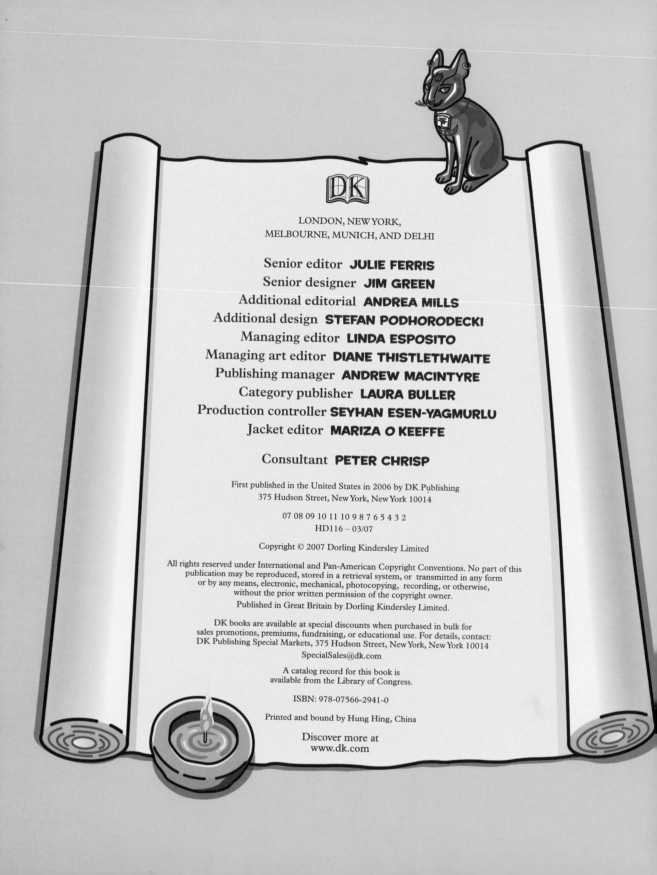

DK

LONDON, NEW YORK,
MELBOURNE, MUNICH, AND DELHI

Senior editor **JULIE FERRIS**
Senior designer **JIM GREEN**
Additional editorial **ANDREA MILLS**
Additional design **STEFAN PODHORODECKI**
Managing editor **LINDA ESPOSITO**
Managing art editor **DIANE THISTLETHWAITE**
Publishing manager **ANDREW MACINTYRE**
Category publisher **LAURA BULLER**
Production controller **SEYHAN ESEN-YAGMURLU**
Jacket editor **MARIZA O KEEFFE**

Consultant **PETER CHRISP**

First published in the United States in 2006 by DK Publishing
375 Hudson Street, New York, New York 10014

07 08 09 10 11 10 9 8 7 6 5 4 3 2
HD116 – 03/07

DK books are available at special discounts when purchased in bulk for
sales promotions, premiums, fundraising, or educational use. For details, contact:
DK Publishing Special Markets, 375 Hudson Street, New York, New York 10014
SpecialSales@dk.com

A catalog record for this book is
available from the Library of Congress.

ISBN: 978-07566-2941-0

Printed and bound by Hung Hing, China

Discover more at
www.dk.com

CONTENTS

Get this thing off my head, I can't read the contents!

Enter the Egyptians

The Ancient Egyptians are super-cool dudes. They build one of the most important civilizations and are among the first to use writing and develop a calendar. Ruled by a king called the pharaoh, they have an awesome religion with loads of gods and goddesses. They also build incredible temples and monuments. For 3,000 years, these dudes rock!

Egypt is a dry, desert land on the north coast of Africa. The mighty Nile River flows through the desert on its way to the Mediterranean Sea. Every year, the river floods, leaving behind rich soil for farming. These dudes grow wheat, barley, grapes, figs, and all kinds of vegetables here. That's awesome considering they are smack in the middle of a desert. On the plus side, the desert protects the Egyptians. Nasty invaders are put off by the harsh location—cool.

What's the point?

The Egyptians are master builders and architects. They put up huge stone temples and big pyramid tombs. These are the pyramids at Giza, one of which houses the body of Pharaoh Khufu.

Capital idea

The town of Memphis becomes the capital when the Upper and Lower kingdoms of Egypt unite. A holy cow lives there—the Apis bull. He may look like a cud-chewer, but he is actually a real live god. No bull!

Fertile farmland

Egyptians owe everything to the Nile River. Every year, it floods. When the waters retreat, a fertile black soil is left behind that is fantastic for growing. Farmer dudes can grow almost everything they need, thanks to the river.

Sun-worshipper

Pharaoh Akhenaten worships the sun, instead of the gods and goddesses. He builds a new town at Amarna and a temple where he can catch rays and give praise. When he dies, the city is abandoned.

Rock stars

Some of the stone temples really rock. Abu Simbel, built by Rameses the Great in Nubia, is carved out of a mountain. Four gigantic statues of the pharaoh guard the door.

The Egyptians rely on the river for trading. It's like a highway made of water, dude. Traders also travel to other countries bordering the Mediterranean Sea to snag super-exotic goods. Land routes are more difficult, but these intrepid dudes pack up their donkeys and hit the land anyway, to get stuff they can't grow or make at home.

Trading and farming make Egypt a wealthy country, and the strong governments help keep the peace. People think their pharaoh rulers are the living link between the gods and the regular dudes. When a pharaoh dies, he lives as a god in the afterlife. How spooky is that, dude?

Enough chit-chat from me. You need to meet these desert-taming, Nile-loving, pyramid-building, mummy-making dudes for yourself.

First steps

The master architect Imhotep is the first dude to build a step pyramid at Saqqara. Pharaohs can hop right up the steps to heaven! Neat.

River living

The Nile River serves as a waterway connecting the different bits of the country. Boats zip up and down the river, and Egyptian traders can ply their goods all along the Nile.

Crowning glory

Thebes replaces Memphis as the new capital of Egypt, and the government operates from here. The pharaoh is head of the government. He wears a red and white double crown for official occasions.

Karnak

The fantastic temple of Karnak is the world's largest religious site. The Egyptians have about 2,000 gods and goddesses. Some are worshipped all across Egypt, while others have regional followings.

Farming dudes

Forget the palaces and temples—Egypt's real wealth lies in the rich farmlands by the Nile. Almost everyone is involved in agriculture (fancy name for farming), from peasants hoeing the fields to landowners counting the profits. How does a country surrounded by desert produce anything but sand? The secret is in the yearly flooding of the Nile, and the fertile earth left when the river retreats.

The farm year has three seasons. The first is *akhet*—the time of the flood. Every year, rain in the Ethiopia highlands pours into the Nile. In June, the surging water reaches Egypt. The river overflows and the farmlands on its banks are completely submerged.

The second season is *peret*—the time of planting and growth. When the fields are dry enough to walk across without sinking in, farmers get busy. They mark out the boundaries between their fields and build dykes (walls made of piled-up earth) on top of them. The government sends scribes to make careful records of who farms where, so they know how much tax to claim after the harvest. Typical. Ditches are dug down between the marked-off plots of land to trap the remaining flood water. The farmer will use it to water his crops later on.

To loosen up the soil and get it ready for planting, farmers hook plows to a pair of oxen and criss-cross the fields. After a few times, the soil is broken up into manageable chunks. Then, farmers loosen the chunks of soil even more with hoes. It's back-breaking work, dude.

Sometime around March or April, the crops are ready to harvest. It is *shomu*—the time of harvest and drought. Of course, the first thing that happens is the government scribe turns up again. The nosey little dude wants to check the crops and ensure the government gets its slice of the pie. The harvest is the busiest time of the year. Everyone has to pitch in. There are celebrations to honor and thank the gods of the harvest, and then it's time to bring in the crops.

I knew I shouldn't have stuck my oar in!

The harvesters advance along the field of grain in rows, hacking the ears of grain with flint-bladed sickles. The stalks are collected to make straw for the animals. Dudettes and brats comb the newly cut fields looking for ears of grain the dudes have missed.

Farmers keep watch on the rising river. If the flooding is minor, the water may not reach all the fields. If there is too much water, it will destroy the fields and may sweep away animals and villages. Eek! During the flood, dudes repair farm equipment and tools, and make sure storage buildings are in top shape. Lazier dudes choose the flood season to goof off a little. By November, the waters have retreated, leaving a layer of silt (a rich mud). Now it's time to get to work. Damn.

Once the soil is ready, the seeds are sown, including grains such as wheat and barley, and loads of veggies. The seed sower walks up and down the field, chucking seeds out of a basket. Goats or pigs are let loose to trample the seeds into the ground. The farmer weeds and waters the growing crops.

The husks and stalks of the grain (chaff) are separated from the edible kernels by threshing. Grain is laid out and trampled on by cows to open the husks and release the kernels. Dudettes toss the grain in the air, so the light chaff blows away, and the good stuff is left.

Home, sweet home

Brats running around, the cat underfoot, and housework piling up—it's an ordinary day for this Egyptian peasant family. They live in a small, cozy home built of mud bricks. Most of the work takes place in an open courtyard, and the rooms for living are at the back. Let's sneak a peek inside while they're not looking.

Pick up your toys, or they're going in the Nile!

Women weave thread into cloth on looms.

Making a meal of it

Food is cooked outside when possible, so there's less risk of fire. These dudes can't afford meat, but the Nile is full of fish. Bread and beer are the mealtime staples. Dudettes grind grain into flour, mix it with water to make dough, and slap blobs of it on the outside of a clay oven to make bread. Veggies and fruits finish the menu.

Woven wardrobe

A dude's wardrobe is created at home by the women, who've mastered making cloth. Flax plants are crushed into a tangle of fibers, which is spun into thread. This thread is woven into cloth on a loom.

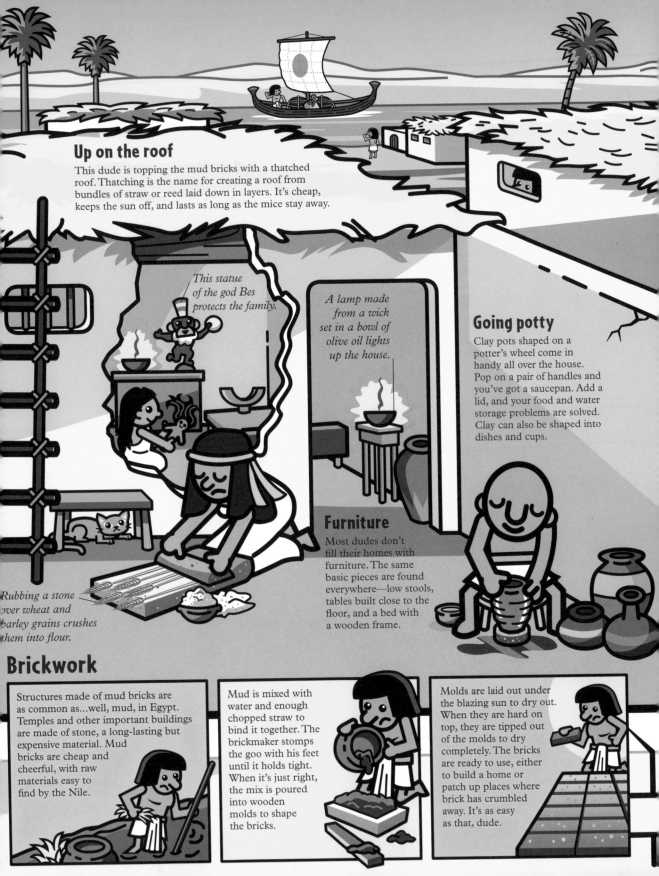

Up on the roof

This dude is topping the mud bricks with a thatched roof. Thatching is the name for creating a roof from bundles of straw or reed laid down in layers. It's cheap, keeps the sun off, and lasts as long as the mice stay away.

This statue of the god Bes protects the family.

A lamp made from a wick set in a bowl of olive oil lights up the house.

Going potty

Clay pots shaped on a potter's wheel come in handy all over the house. Pop on a pair of handles and you've got a saucepan. Add a lid, and your food and water storage problems are solved. Clay can also be shaped into dishes and cups.

Rubbing a stone over wheat and barley grains crushes them into flour.

Furniture

Most dudes don't fill their homes with furniture. The same basic pieces are found everywhere—low stools, tables built close to the floor, and a bed with a wooden frame.

Brickwork

Structures made of mud bricks are as common as...well, mud, in Egypt. Temples and other important buildings are made of stone, a long-lasting but expensive material. Mud bricks are cheap and cheerful, with raw materials easy to find by the Nile.

Mud is mixed with water and enough chopped straw to bind it together. The brickmaker stomps the goo with his feet until it holds tight. When it's just right, the mix is poured into wooden molds to shape the bricks.

Molds are laid out under the blazing sun to dry out. When they are hard on top, they are tipped out of the molds to dry completely. The bricks are ready to use, either to build a home or patch up places where brick has crumbled away. It's as easy as that, dude.

Noble living

Nestled by the Nile and oozing with style, this wealthy nobleman's family home is a totally killer villa. The large, luxurious house is set among gorgeous grounds, encircled by a high wall for privacy. Everything a dude could wish for, from a beautiful garden to chill in, to a shrine to worship in, is found within the villa walls. Like many simpler homes, this mini-mansion is built with bricks of sun-dried mud, but these down-to-earth ingredients make for an incredibly posh pad.

1 The main entrance is through this towered gate in the wall. A gatekeeper checks visitors in.

2 They say the family that prays together, stays together, and this family worships at their own shrine.

3 Check out this beauty spot. With a great garden and lavish pool, this dude must be loaded.

4 There's plenty to do, so lots of servants live and work within the villa walls.

5 Walls are built using the Nile's thick mud, smoothed with plaster, and painted in light colors.

6 Grain for the household and animals is stored in these mini-domes.

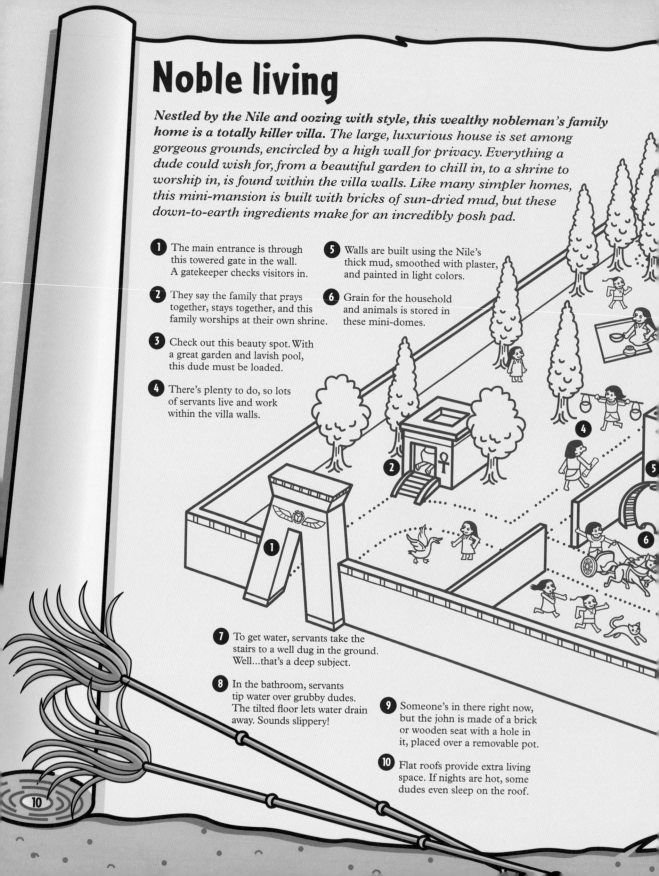

7 To get water, servants take the stairs to a well dug in the ground. Well...that's a deep subject.

8 In the bathroom, servants tip water over grubby dudes. The tilted floor lets water drain away. Sounds slippery!

9 Someone's in there right now, but the john is made of a brick or wooden seat with a hole in it, placed over a removable pot.

10 Flat roofs provide extra living space. If nights are hot, some dudes even sleep on the roof.

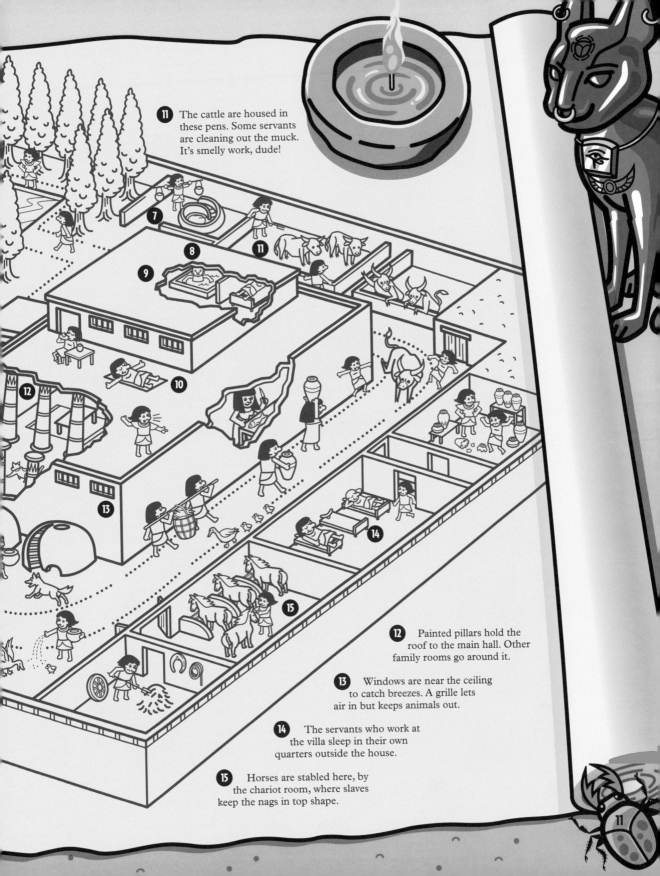

11 The cattle are housed in these pens. Some servants are cleaning out the muck. It's smelly work, dude!

12 Painted pillars hold the roof to the main hall. Other family rooms go around it.

13 Windows are near the ceiling to catch breezes. A grille lets air in but keeps animals out.

14 The servants who work at the villa sleep in their own quarters outside the house.

15 Horses are stabled here, by the chariot room, where slaves keep the nags in top shape.

Party on, dude

Those Egyptians really know how to throw a party. Good music, good food, and good people make really good times, dude. Some parties are to celebrate an event—maybe a great harvest, a wedding, or the birth of a brat. On banquet day, the party room is filled with flowers. Everyone wears their best clothes (and wigs), the host lays on fine food and drink, and musicians get the house rocking. Let's get the party started.

Welcome to the banquet. The guests arrive in their most deluxe duds. Everyone wears their brightest whites for special occasions.

Guests are given garlands of flowers, some dudettes tuck blossom in their wigs. The whole scene is fabulous, darling.

Party dudes perch cones of perfumed wax on top of their wigs. As the party hots up, the wax begins to melt. Waxy goo drips down through the wig and into the skin, and the sweet scent of perfume is released. By the time the party hat's melted, the wearer smells amazing.

How about a napkin, idiot?

How about a smooch, dudette?

A party don't mean a thing if it ain't got that swing. Female dancers weave among the guests, swaying to the beat of the music. The dudettes really tear up the dance floor. Sometimes acrobats do tricks to entertain the party crowd. It looks like the joint is really jumping now.

All night long, servants rush around, carrying trays of totally tasty things to eat. Meat is a luxury in Ancient Egypt, but the host spares no expense. There are dishes made of beef, goat, pork, and fish seasoned with spices such as rosemary and garlic.

Platters of garbanzo beans, lentils, and salads are piled high. Yummy breads are served along with butter and cheese, and honeyed figs and other fruits satisfy the sweet tooth. The gorgeous food is washed down with plenty of beer and wine. Hiccup.

Live music is a must. Musicians play stringed instruments (lutes, lyres, and harps), blow flutes, and pound the drums. The room rocks!

Partygoers sit pretty on benches by tables topped with plates and cups. Late into the evening, they nibble and gobble, gossip and guzzle, giggle and flirt. Everyone really lets their hair down, even if they've shaved it off.

Out on the town

The town: it's sizzling hot, it's incredibly noisy, it's way too crowded, and the dust sticks to you like glue. Still, lots of dudes wouldn't live anywhere else. The market down on the dockside is a great place to snag a bargain, and the local shops are filled with excellent goods.

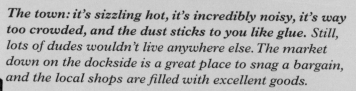

Everything you need

The town's shops and workshops are found at the street level. There are brewers, bakers, cloth-makers, carpenter's workshops, tool repair shops, and pottery shops.

River view

Space is hard to come by in town, and everyone is after that amazing river view, so the buildings are tall and narrow. The buildings are two or three stories high, constructed of mud bricks.

The riverbank

Need to cool off after a spot of shopping, and escape the heat of the day? Pop down to the riverside. It's much cooler down by the water. Don't be tempted to dangle your toes in the water, though, because there are hungry crocodiles around.

Sun screen

The outer walls of the houses are whitewashed (slapped with a coat or two of a chalky white paint) to help deflect the intense rays of the sun and keep the buildings as cool as possible.

What a dump!

There is no garbage collection or sewage system. Waste of all kinds is taken outside and dumped in garbage pits, the river, or right on the street. Careful where you walk!

A weighty issue

Traders use a set of scales to weigh copper nuggets known as *deben*. Each item is given a value based on a certain weight in *deben*, so trades are fair and square.

Meet me at the market

Traders spread their mats on the banks of the river, lay out their goods, and get ready to haggle. Most dudes grow their own food and make their own cloth. But if they have extra stuff to spare, they might as well trade it for something new.

Getting around

Nipping up and down the Nile on a boat is the easiest and fastest way to get around. Traders who live outside the city get their goods to market this way. Loading up the family donkey is another way to transport stuff, but not so much fun for the donkey.

Dude fashion

Wigs
Hair is shaved off or kept short because of the sweltering temperatures. Dudes don wigs at parties or special events.

Kilts
For basic daily wear, men wear linen kilts tied at the waist. Try one with a shoulder strap if you're worried about drooping. Got a tough job to do? Wear a loincloth, as seen on our male model.

Jewelry
Everyone loves jewelry. Armlets, anklets, pendants, and collars—you can never have too much, dude.

Tunics
A nobleman might wear a loose top known as a tunic over his kilt. He glams up the look with a glitzy collar.

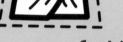

Animal skins
What's new, pussycat? Priests or pharaohs wear animal skins for ceremonies and big events. Leopardskin is the hottest look.

It's hot in Egypt, but you can still look cool. Here's the latest in dude fashion. This season (and every season) it's all about linen. This fabric, made from fibers of the flax plant, is ideal for hot weather.

Sandals
If you're dressing up, reach for the sandals. Barefoot is so last year, dude.

Eye, eye
Egyptians circle their eyes with dark make-up called kohl. They make it by mixing dark-colored minerals with oil in a little pot. The kohl is painted around the eyelids with a small stick. A kohl-rimmed eye looks super cool and helps shade the eyes from the harsh glare of the sun. Glam eyes, a spritz of perfume, and a dab of oil to keep the skin moist...you're looking good, dude.

A bit on the side
Little dudes usually run around in their birthday suits, although some dress up in mini versions of the clothes their parents wear. Rug rats shave off all the hair on their heads except for a long ponytail to one side. This sidelock is worn as a sign of youth. Boys and girls wear sidelocks until they hit puberty. That's when the zits arrive.

Dudette fashion

Wigs

For big dos, pop on a wig and your hair is done. A perfume hair cone atop your wig is a must-have. The cone contains perfumed wax, and as it starts to melt, dudettes smell sweet.

Fans

Are you sweating from the sizzle? Cool things down a little with this feather fan.

Jewelry

Gold, silver, gemstones, colored glass: bring on the bling, sister.

Tunics

Cover your shoulders with this shawl-like tunic. Layering is so on-trend.

Collars

Dudettes can't go wrong with a collar. It tops off your tunic, and comes in a variety of colors.

Grooming

Mirror, mirror in my hand. Who's the cutest in the land? That would be you. See for yourself in a shiny copper mirror.

Sandals

Keep it simple with sandals. Not only are they the number one shoe style for dudettes, but your tootsies get some air, too.

Calling all Egyptian fashionistas! Do you want a look that is hotter than July? Here you go. Start with a straight linen dress, try layering with tunics, then pile on the bling. A great wig will fix your hairdo.

Pluck and preen

In a hot place, it's really important to wash regularly to keep fresh as a lotus. Egyptians take a dip in the river, or wash up with a bowlful of water poured from a jug. Rich people have foot baths to soak stinky toes, and the super-posh have rooms in their houses where servants douse them with water. As part of the bathing routine, women shave their legs with razors. Pay attention...no nicks, please!

Pleat process

To make super-fancy clothes, linen can be pressed into even folds called pleats. The fabric is soaked in water, then the damp linen is pressed into a board cut with deep, even grooves, and left to dry. The linen is lifted from the board and the pleats are sewn down to keep them in place. Pleated fabric is especially popular with dudettes who party.

17

At the Wigmaker's

Looking cool is really important in Ancient Egypt and a hot hairdo is key to a good look—Egyptian hair can never be too black or too bountiful. So, what if your locks are lacking? Off with the old hair and on with the new: a wig, especially crafted for you. Let's book an appointment at the wigmaker's shop and find out more.

Q: *Who wears wigs?*

A: Both men and women get wiggy. Most Egyptians keep their hair short or shave it all off, and here's why. First, it is so blazing hot in Egypt that a bare head is much more comfortable. Second, a crop top is much easier to keep clean and free of head lice. Third, you can change your whole look with a wig swap. And last but not least, the quality and style of your wig lets everyone know your place in the world. Wealthy people might have lots of wigs, and really ritzy rugs for special occasions.

Q: *Who makes the wigs? What materials do they use?*

A: Barbers and specialist wigmakers are in charge of crafting wigs. Wigmaking is a respectable job and wigs vary in quality and price. The top-of-the range hairpieces are made entirely of human hair. Midpriced wigs are made of human hair mixed in with plant fibers (often from palm trees) or wool. In the bargain bin are wigs made entirely of plant fibers. Dyes give the wigs the jet-black color favored by Egyptians. The wigs can also be styled with curls, twirls, or waves—whatever is the fashion of the day. And, of course, they are essential for the afterlife, so the dead are buried in the tombs with their wigs.

> I'll take care of these split ends.

> Come back you cheeky monkey...

How the wigs are made...

Egyptian wig-crafting is a real art. First, plant fibers (such as leaves from a palm tree) are used to make a close-fitting cap to fit the subject's head. But wigmakers can't just *leaf* well enough alone. They have to add fake hair.

Dyed human hair (or a mix of human hair, plant fibers, and sheep's wool) is bundled into strands. Then the strands of hair are shaped. They may be cut, twisted, curled, or braided. Some strands are left long, while others are cut to make shorter wigs.

Each strand is attached to the cap with melted beeswax or resin (the sticky stuff that comes from pine trees). Some wigs are simple with only a few layers. Others are built up layer by layer until they are super full. Now that's a hairstyle and a half.

18

Q: *Do dudes wear their wigs all the time? What do they do when they are off their heads? The wigs, that is.*

A: Even though dudes are happy to shave their heads, they don't walk around bald (even when no one is looking). Wigs are worn most of the time, both inside and outside the house. (Priests, however, go for the chrome-dome look 24/7.) When not in use, wigs are kept in special boxes on wig stands. The off-duty barnets are combed, rubbed with special oils made from vegetable or animal fats to keep them in good condition, and scented with smelly spices or fragrant wood chips, so they are good to go for the next wearing.

Q: *Do nippers wear wigs?*

A: No, but most young dudes wear their hair in one style until they become teenagers. The head is shaved apart from one long strand left at the side of the head. This s-shaped lock of hair looks like the hieroglyphic symbol for child or youth.

Q: *So everyone is happy to pop on a wig in Egypt?*

A: No one is bothered if you can see a little skull stubble or a dude's real hair underneath the wig—it is far worse for others to think you can't afford a wig in the first place.

Doctor dude

If it ain't broke, don't fix it, but if it is broke, and it's your leg, you'd better drag yourself to the doctor. Egyptian doctors are the best around. Some dudes travel from abroad to see one. Doctors use a mix of medicine and magic. Practical treatments, such as herbs and potions, relieve pain and other symptoms. Spells get rid of bad spirits that cause illness, so the patient is cured. The waiting room's this way.

> Take a break from work.

> Eye of Horus, open wide this place of seeing!

Broken bones

This pyramid-builder's arm broke, so the doctor rubs in a soothing mix of oil and honey. He puts a wood support under the arm to keep the bone still, and holds it with a bandage, tucking an Eye of Horus amulet inside. Job done.

Blurred vision

This poor guy has a cataract in his eye. The lens is so cloudy he can barely see. Maybe it's a good thing because the doctor's about to mash up tortoise brains with honey and put the goop on the eye, while chanting a spell to Horus.

> Don't burn me with the bill!

> Hail Eye of Horus ointment! Bring your healing powers to repair this sorry hand!

Skin sizzle

The next patient was burned when an oil lamp overturned. The doctor mixes up a potion of mother's milk, sticky gum from a tree, and ram's hair. He recites a magic spell as he covers the burn with the ointment. Don't try this at home.

Headbanger

The pounding! The aching! The agony! This guy has a splitting headache. The doc gives the dude some relaxing myrrh and milk, then spits on his head four times. He talks to the pain, dude. In no time, the patient gets his head together.

Blocked passage

It's been a whole week since this dude has had a poo. He needs unblocking, fast. While shouting a spell, the doctor blends some slippery castor oil with beer. As soon as the drink is downed, the dude rushes to the latrine before the floodgates open.

Tailwind

The last patient is here, and dude does he have bad gas! Holding his nose, the doctor gives him crushed dill seeds in beer to calm the digestive system. He breathes a sigh of relief as his office shuts for the day.

Peg pain

Doctors even deal with dental problems. This dude has the toothache from hell. The doctor squishes garlic (an antiseptic that kills bacteria) into vinegar and water, and slaps it on the gums. The dude now has killer bad breath, but the tooth won't be infected.

21

Ready, Sed, go!

When a pharaoh has been ruler for a terrific 30 years, he deserves a party, right dude? Say a banquet to end all banquets? Or a super-deluxe Nile cruise? Even better, how about running around a track carrying stuff with a crown balanced on his head? That's the ticket! Welcome to the Sed festival. Let's cheer on the pharaoh.

Dude, are you really fit to be pharaoh?

The pharaoh has lots of rituals to perform. After 30 years in power, and then every three years afterward, he runs a race to mark the Sed festival (named after a jackal god). The festival helps restore his powers, so he can carry on ruling—if he ever gets his breath back.

The pharaoh reaches the finish line! The crowd goes wild. The pharaoh sits on a pair of thrones and is carried off to a party. The dude is wiped out. He'll need three years to recover.

22

Upper Egypt

Before 3000 B.C. Egypt is split into two kingdoms—Upper Egypt in the south and Lower Egypt in the north. The pharaoh of Upper Egypt wears a tall white crown.

Lower Egypt

The ruler of Lower Egypt wears a chair-shaped red crown. When Upper Egypt conquers Lower Egypt, the lands are joined. The pharaoh wears both crowns combined.

The course goes around stones that represent Egypt. Guests lucky enough to snag an invite are excited. Most dudes see the Sed once in their lifetimes, if that. The pharaoh makes an offering, dons the white crown of Upper Egypt, holds a pair of sacred cups, and he's off!

Go, pharaoh, go! He's whizzing around the track and he's reached the last lap. Surely this race will restore his power, bring harmony to the universe, and ensure he rules for as long in the next life.

Costume change! After four trips around the course in the white crown of Upper Egypt, it's time to switch to the red crown of Lower Egypt. He holds an emblem of royalty—the flail (a sort of whip). That dude is whipping around the track. How does he do it, at his age? What a guy.

23

Who's who in Egypt?

In a society, you've got to follow the rules if you want to live together, work together, and generally get along. But who has the power to make the rules? And who makes sure people follow them? This pyramid (naturally) of people shows who's got the power in Egypt. From the big cats at the top of the pyramid to the peasant population at the bottom, everyone has a role to play. The difference is, some have starring roles, and others are more like extras.

Vizier

After the pharaoh, the main dude in government is the vizier. He keeps an eye on things, counting up people and making sure they pay taxes, signing off on property deals, and keeping track of valuables.

Priests

These dudes work in the temples to serve the gods. The temple scribes that work alongside the priests can read and write and help with government duties like recordkeeping.

Governors

Egypt is divided into 42 nomes (like counties). A nomarch (governor) runs each nome, keeps an archive of records, and reports back to the vizier. These dudes are often mates or relatives of the pharaoh.

Mayors

The mayors are in charge of the small towns and provinces within the nomes. These dudes let the nomarchs know what's going on in their neck of the woods, and make sure the locals follow the rules set by the central government.

Village elders

In towns too teeny for a mayor, the elders are in charge as local representatives of the government. Like the mayors, they work for the nomarch and carry out the orders of the central government.

Peasants

The biggest group of dudes are the ones who raise the cattle, farm the fields, fish the river, make the crafts, build the temples, and, most importantly, pay the taxes.

Pharaoh

There is no question about who's at the top of the heap:
the pharaoh is the dude with absolute power. He's also so
holy he can talk to the gods. Awesome. He is in charge of
the government and decides what actions to take.

Chief priest

Of course, the pharaoh is the holiest and highest
priest in the land, but he can't be everywhere at
once. He turns over some of his religious duties
to the priests, especially the chief priest.

Commander-in-chief

The pharaoh is the ultimate head of the army and
may lead the army into battle himself, but he can
turn over day-to-day control of the military to a
commander—usually his son or a trusted relative.

Army

Under the command of the…
er, commander, the army is led
by generals and less powerful
officers, and staffed by brave
men who like adventure. If
you can dodge the arrows, it is
not a bad job. There is plenty
of action, and sometimes
captured booty is shared out.

Scribe school

You can't remember everything, dude. With all the laws, spells, and records, you've got to write it down. Egyptians believe writing is a gift from Thoth, god of wisdom, so they call their script medu neter—the word of the gods. We know it as hieroglyphics—sacred writings. Dudes who learn to write well are called scribes. These boys are learning to write at scribe school. If they mind their p's and q's, they get jobs at the temple or with the government. If they goof around, let's just say the writing's on the wall.

Arm

Reed

Vulture

Jar stand

Owl

Foot

Flax

Animal belly

Door bolt

Mat

Crown

Bull

Rope

Snake

Sloping hill

House

Basket

Loaf

Hand

Horned viper

Sun

Bar

Pool

Celebration

Mouth

Water

Child

Courtyard

Write on, dude

Scribes write on scrolls of paper made from papyrus leaves. It's not cheap, so for note-scribbling, they write on pieces of broken pottery. A scribe's writing kit is an ivory box called a palette. It holds brushes made of reeds and pots of ink. Scribes must learn more than 1,000 picture signs. Each one stands for the sound of a letter, or for a word or an action. Characters can go left to right, right to left, or up and down. The pictures tell you which way to read. If animals or dudes face left, you read from left to right. If they're looking right, you read right to left. If they're looking right at you, you're paranoid.

Man

Woman

Walk

River

Wood

Lion

Lasso

Chick

Cloth

27

Temple priest

Priests are very important religious dudes in ancient Egypt. People believe that the gods live among them, in temples. Each temple is built to honor a particular god. In a super-sacred room deep inside the temple where only the priests can go, there is a statue of the god. The priests talk to the statue to get messages to and from the god. Let's tag along with a temple dude to find out more.

Q: *Hi dude. This temple is really amazing. Can you tell us about it?*

A: Can do, dude. You go in through a gateway called a pylon. There are two columns outside called obelisks. They are monuments to the sun god. Inside, there's a grand courtyard—on special occasions you may get to see that. The rest of the temple is strictly off limits to ordinary dudes.

Q: *Bummer. Can you tell us what's in there? Pretty please?*

A: OK, you twisted my arm. Next there's a special room called the hypostyle hall. It's dark and full of columns carved to look like papyrus plants. When light enters, the columns look like they are blooming in the sun. Awesome!

Me with the other priests, carrying the god. Say cheese!

Isn't this mural totally awesome?

Sanctuary

Second hall

Hypostyle hall

Pylon Obelisk

We use the hypostyle hall for religious rituals. These are different ways to honor the god.

Q: *So where does the god live?*

A: His home is the sanctuary. It's the coolest part of the temple, hands down. The walls feature mysterious murals starring the god. The statue of the god sits in a special box called a shrine.

Most temples look like this one. The gods designed the first one, and we copied it.

Courtyard

28

Q: *Cool. I've heard that looking after the statue is your biggest job. Can you tell us what that involves?*

A: Well, first thing every morning, the high priest breaks the clay seal on the sanctuary doors. He goes in, lights some incense, and says prayers to the god. We want to awaken its spirit so it protects us. Then he washes it and dresses it in clothing and jewels. We put a bang-up breakfast nearby as an offering to the god. We want to thank him and let him know we're taking care of him. Who knows what trouble might befall us if we stop feeding the god? I certainly don't want to find out.

Q: *Tell us a little bit more about you. How did you get this top job? Do you live here, too?*

A: The pharaoh picks us, or the job is handed down to us by a member of our family. It's not a full-time job. We may be on duty for a month, then off for two. We live in a house on the temple grounds when it's our turn to serve. Before we start work, we must wash in a sacred pool, shave all our hair off, and sniff incense to clean our bodies and clear our heads. We can wear linen, leopard skins, or cloth made from plants. Loads of other people are hard at work in the temple.

Priests from other temples drop by, but that hippo's not coming in!

We put out an amazing spread for the god each day. Yummy.

Q: *What about the rest of the day?*

A: At noon and at dusk there are more prayers, offerings, and songs. We pass along questions and requests dudes have handed to us outside the temple. Sometimes, during religious festivals, we let the dudes get closer to the god by carrying its statue through the streets on a barque. That's a golden boat to you, pal.

There are singers and musicians to make a beautiful noise, scribes to copy down religious writings and prayer requests, and craftspeople who make sacred objects. Busy, busy, busy.

Q: *OK, last one, then you can get back to work. Tell us...what happens to the food?*

A: We eat it, dude.

Apis the Bull

Egyptians believe that certain gods live among them in the bodies of animals. The creator god Ptah comes to Earth as a bull—the Apis. Priests can spot the Apis by markings on its body, but they go through a lot of bull to find him.

Nope, no holy cow here.

After an Apis dies, priests all over Egypt hunt for a baby bull with a white diamond on its forehead, a bird-shaped mark on its back, double tail hairs, and a scarab-shaped mark under its tongue. Eventually…bullseye! It's time to party with the new Apis.

Dude, you're a total god.

The overjoyed Egyptians are ready to rock. (After all, having a real live god around is a pretty big deal.) The new Apis is whisked off to Memphis in a fabulous boat with a custom-built golden cabin. How divine is that?

Fall in… please fall in…

In his temple compound, Apis gets the A-list treatment from the priests. He dines on the best foods, lives in luxury, and is given a harem of the most bodacious bovine beauties around. People so worship that bull. The Apis gets total respect. A waft of his bully breath is believed to cure diseases, and his mere presence is thought to make men more manly.

Mom lives a super-deluxe life in the temple, too. She's considered as sacred as her son, so every day is Mother's Day for her. When she dies, she will be mummified in the same way as Egyptian pharaohs.

Why are all these dudes looking at me?

Like any VID (very important dude), the Apis makes public appearances. Often he sits in a window at the temple so people can gaze at him in all his awesomeness. On special occasions, he struts through the streets of Memphis, bedecked in glitzy accessories. The crowd go nuts—they simply can't get enough of their cool bull.

I could so go for a burger, but they haven't been invented yet.

Dudes also believe the Apis is an oracle, who can answer questions and predict the future through its bullish body language. A worshipper asks a question, Apis strikes a pose, and a priest interprets the answer. (Surely a little bull involved here.)

It is a sad day for everyone when the Apis dies. The Apis is mummified, given a full-on funeral, then buried in the underground catacombs at Saqqara, with mom's mummy. The priests then start the search for the new sacred bull.

Dude, he'll be back.

Myth of Osiris

Egyptian god Osiris has it all. The other gods name him king of the earth, the Egyptians adore him, and his wife Isis is smitten. Yet his brother Seth is not part of the fan club. The jealous dude throws a party, where he shows off a cool chest. He says he'll give it to anyone who fits inside, and Osiris jumps in. Seth shuts the lid and bolts it down. Case closed? We think not...

Seth chucks the chest into the Nile. What a bad dude. The current sweeps it away and carries it out to sea. Eventually it washes up on a faraway beach. Isis has been searching frantically for the box containing her husband. When she finds it, she opens the lid, and tips out Osiris...dead as a doorknob.

My lifeless love! You will live again!

Isis takes the body back to Egypt. She is determined to bring him back to life...but how? She decides to take some time out and sleep on it. While she snoozes, sneaky Seth creeps in, finds Osiris's soggy body, and hacks it into pieces. He scatters the poor dude's body parts all over Egypt. And you thought your brother was mean.

Isis and her sister fly over Egypt looking for bits of Osiris. The trip costs an arm and a leg, but they do find everything. They re-assemble the body and the god of embalming, jackal-headed Anubis, helps them create the first mummy. After a magic spell, Osiris is reborn to rule the dead!

Isis and her mummy-man have a son, Horus. He grows up determined to avenge his father. Horus wants to make his evil uncle Seth, who rules Egypt, pay for killing his dad. The uncle and the nephew fight a totally epic battle. It's so loud that all the other gods wake up. Seth pokes out Horus's eye! Bet he didn't see that coming.

The other gods and goddesses are not best pleased, so they get involved. Super goddess Hathor heals Horus's eye. From then on, the eye symbol represents healing. The gods decide to punish Seth for being such a jerk. They make him the god of deserts and storms—a cool job, but being king is better. They give the throne of Egypt to Horus. Everything is cool.

Mummification

The Egyptians believe that when you die, your soul leaves your body and takes a trip to the underworld. There, Osiris, Lord of the Underworld, names your fate. If he thinks you have been an awesome dude, he welcomes your soul to join him forever in his underworld kingdom. But Egyptians believe that souls still need bodies to live in, so the dead dude must be preserved as a mummy. Here's how a dead pharaoh is turned into a wrap star.

Mummy-making is a ritual and there are things the embalmers must do at each stage. Shortly after the pharaoh bites the dust, his body is taken to a tent called the *ibu* (place of purification). The body gets a good scrubbing with water mixed with natron—salty stuff mined from lake beds near the Nile.

Brains are useless anyway.

I don't think I can stomach this.

The squeaky-clean body is moved to a tent called the *per nefer* (house of beauty). A helper sticks a hook up the nose to the brain, pokes it until it turns into brain soup, then turns the body on its side to drain out the ooze.

A priest wearing the jackal mask of Anubis (the god of death) marks a line down the body. A helper cuts along the line, and the dog-headed dude goes barking mad and chases him out of the room for harming an Egyptian. This is all part of the ritual.

The liver, stomach, intestines, and lungs are removed. (The heart stays put because the Egyptians think it is the center of intelligence.) The organs are washed, packed in natron to dry them out, wrapped up, and placed in containers called canopic jars.

Bacteria-ridden fluids lead to decay, so the body has to dry out completely. The pharaoh's body is buried under a giant pile of natron and left to dry for 40 days. Then it is washed, packed out with bags of sawdust, rubbed in oils, dusted with spices, and coated in hot pine resin to seal everything.

Why live forever if you aren't going to look like a yummy mummy? A make-up artist adds cosmetics to make the body look more lifelike. Sometimes onions are stuck under the eyelids to make fake eyeballs. The hole in the side of the body is sewn up and covered with a wax or copper plate decorated as the Eye of Horus.

Around 50 days after the dude's death, the body is wrapped up in strips of fine linen. Ten fingers and ten toes are wrapped individually. Each limb is bandaged separately, too, as well as the head. Big sheets of linen that envelop the whole body are frequently added.

Between the layers of linen, mummy-makers place special amulets (magical jewelry) to help protect the body on its journey to the afterlife. As the mummy is wrapped, a priest reads spells out loud to help ward off evil. The arms and legs are tied together, and a scroll of the *Book of the Dead* (a kind of afterlife city guide) is placed between the mummy's hands. Bandaging takes about two weeks, then, it's a wrap! Well, almost…

The dried-out, wrapped-up dude is given a final coat of resin and a mask to cover his face, then he's laid in a coffin painted with his portrait, so the soul will have no trouble spotting it. The embalmers have done the best they can to help the body and soul unite.

The long goodbye

With the show over for the pharaoh dude, his mummified body is left for three months, and craftsmen add final touches to the tomb. The funeral procession starts at the royal palace. It's a spectacular show, befitting a pharaoh's last journey on Earth. Family and friends weep, professional mourners wail, and priests make music as the long line of dudes heads to the pharaoh's tomb. The guy in charge is the priest in the leopardskin cloak. He's the pharaoh's son, so he will take over from his father. But today, all that matters is giving his dad a super send-off to the next world.

Major mourners

Leading the mourners is the new pharaoh and family members and friends. Government officials and other important dudes also jump to the front of the line. Professional mourners are hired to get some noise at the funeral. These wailing women make a truly miserable sound and they tear out their hair by the handful—ouch. Priests trudge along, burning incense and jangling their rattles called *sistrums*. It's an eye-popping parade, dude.

Sleigh ride

The pharaoh's mummy rides to the tomb on a fancy sleigh, sometimes built in the shape of a boat. Mourners, or a team of oxen, drag the sleigh along, and get a great upper body workout in the process. Another team follows behind, pulling a second sleigh. This one holds a chest of canopic jars—containers filled with the pharaoh's preserved inner organs. He'll need these back for his next life.

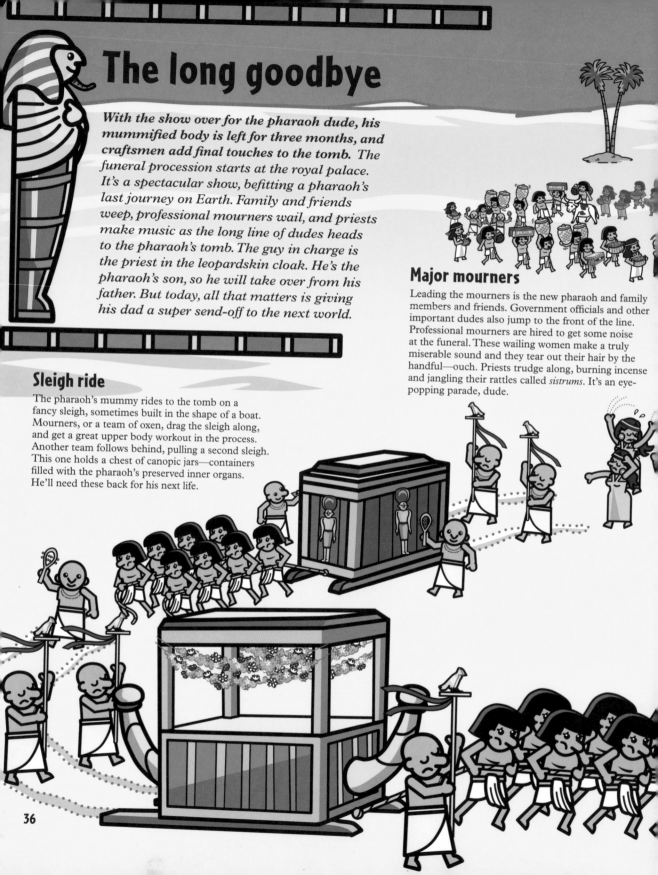

Stuff for the next world

Next in line is a group of dudes carrying furniture, household goods, food, clothing, and the like. You may think they're off to a garage sale, but this stuff belongs to the dead pharaoh. It's all going to the tomb so he has everything he needs to live comfortably in the next life.

Laid to rest

We're here! At the tomb, the coffin is stood upright and the priest performs a special ceremony to help bring the dead pharaoh back to life. The pharaoh's son says his final prayers, and the coffin is placed inside a sarcophagus (large, decorative stone coffin) deep in the tomb's burial chamber. The lid goes down and the burial chamber is sealed with wax or clay. From now on, it's out of this world.

Wake up, dead dude

In a ceremony called "Opening the Mouth," the pharaoh's son performs special rites to wake the dead pharaoh for the next world. There are lots of magic spells, but mostly he touches the mummy with objects, such as a bull's leg, and rubs in oils. Cool.

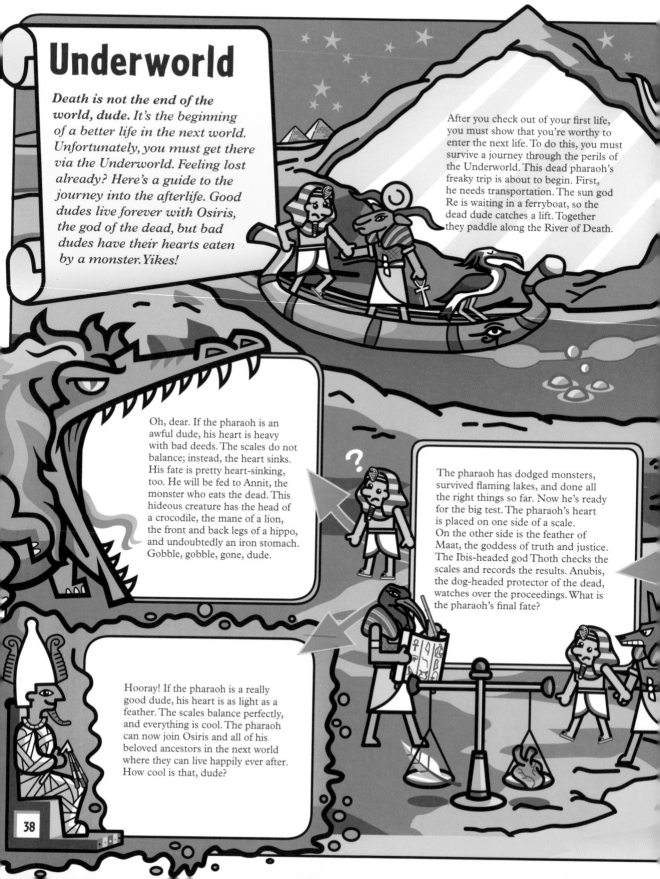

Underworld

Death is not the end of the world, dude. It's the beginning of a better life in the next world. Unfortunately, you must get there via the Underworld. Feeling lost already? Here's a guide to the journey into the afterlife. Good dudes live forever with Osiris, the god of the dead, but bad dudes have their hearts eaten by a monster. Yikes!

After you check out of your first life, you must show that you're worthy to enter the next life. To do this, you must survive a journey through the perils of the Underworld. This dead pharaoh's freaky trip is about to begin. First, he needs transportation. The sun god Re is waiting in a ferryboat, so the dead dude catches a lift. Together they paddle along the River of Death.

Oh, dear. If the pharaoh is an awful dude, his heart is heavy with bad deeds. The scales do not balance; instead, the heart sinks. His fate is pretty heart-sinking, too. He will be fed to Annit, the monster who eats the dead. This hideous creature has the head of a crocodile, the mane of a lion, the front and back legs of a hippo, and undoubtedly an iron stomach. Gobble, gobble, gone, dude.

The pharaoh has dodged monsters, survived flaming lakes, and done all the right things so far. Now he's ready for the big test. The pharaoh's heart is placed on one side of a scale. On the other side is the feather of Maat, the goddess of truth and justice. The Ibis-headed god Thoth checks the scales and records the results. Anubis, the dog-headed protector of the dead, watches over the proceedings. What is the pharaoh's final fate?

Hooray! If the pharaoh is a really good dude, his heart is as light as a feather. The scales balance perfectly, and everything is cool. The pharaoh can now join Osiris and all of his beloved ancestors in the next world where they can live happily ever after. How cool is that, dude?

The Underworld is about as creepy as it gets, dude. It's dark, dismal, and downright dangerous. The place is packed with terrifying monsters, from winged snakes to double-headed, fire-breathing cobras. These crazy carnivorous critters have a taste for human flesh, no matter if it is dead and mummified. Are we there yet?

To help him through the Underworld, the pharaoh turns to his guidebook for the recently deceased, the *Book of the Dead*. This handy papyrus scroll contains maps, helpful hints, lists of spells, and ways to avoid the worst horrors of the Underworld. There are no restaurant reviews, but everything else he needs to know is here. The dude's on a roll now.

Whatever next? The pharaoh encounters several gods along the way. He calls them all by name, to show he is a truly religious dude and rack up some good scores for himself. The gods and goddesses, including this lion-headed gal called Sekhmet, ask him questions, and he must reply correctly. It's a bit like school, only much, much scarier.

Here comes peril! There are loads of trouble spots in the Underworld, meant to challenge the dead dude. This one is high up on the list—a bubbling, boiling lake of fire. Giant snakes having hissy fits and deadly crocodiles with hungry tums pop their ugly heads up through the sizzling surface. The pharaoh makes like a tree and leaves.

Imhotep

Incredible architect, trailblazing astronomer, talented scribe, dedicated doctor, fabulous poet: is there anything this dude cannot do? Imhotep's day job is advisor to Pharaoh Djoser. One day, while brainstorming some plans for Djoser's tomb (not that he wishes the guy dead or anything), he dreams up a super-spectacular structure—the pyramid. Let's meet this genius and find out where he gets his ideas.

Q: *Thank you for giving us a few moments of your very precious time, Imhotep. You could probably be thinking up another one of your great ideas instead, so we are truly grateful.*

A: No trouble at all, young dude. One always needs to make time for his fans. I was once one of the little people too, you know.

Q: *No way. Are you telling me you had humble beginnings?*

A: Oh yes, very much so. I was born in the suburbs, just another commoner. But I'm afraid I couldn't hide my light under a barrel for very long, you know. Whatever I did, I did extremely well. I am blessed with an abundance of natural talents, you see. Some people have even mentioned the "g" word.

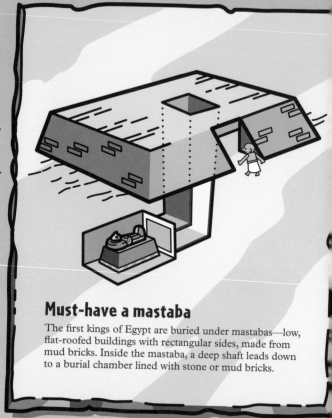

Must-have a mastaba

The first kings of Egypt are buried under mastabas—low, flat-roofed buildings with rectangular sides, made from mud bricks. Inside the mastaba, a deep shaft leads down to a burial chamber lined with stone or mud bricks.

Q: *Godlike?*

A: I was thinking genius, but I can see where you're coming from. Anyway, I rose up the ranks pretty quickly and made quite a name for myself.

Q: *You seem to be a dude of all trades.*

A: Yes, and master of every one! I dabble in a number of fields and of course am rather excellent at all of them. I love philosophy and poetry—so good for the soul. I adore stargazing and astronomy. Don't you wonder what's up there? I do have my religious side and have served as both a scribe and priest. But my real loves are medicine and architecture.

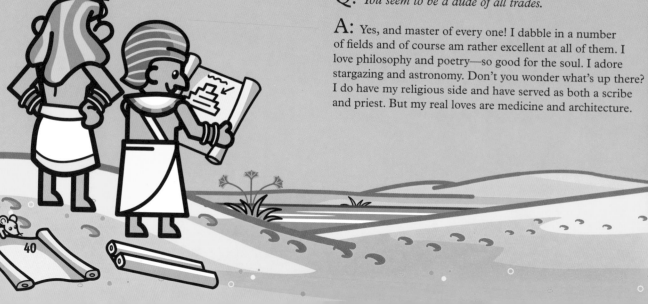

As high priest of the town of Heliopolis, Imhotep is one of the key priests in Egypt. Bow down to that.

This dude never has his head in the clouds. He's a keen astronomer, who studies the night sky.

When you call for a doctor, call for Imhotep. He's treated more than 200 diseases! What a miracle worker.

Imhotep can write and read hieroglyphics and is a trained scribe. Handy for shopping lists.

Q: *I've heard you have written a medical journal that's really helped other doctors understand the way the body works.*

A: Oh, yes. Ailments, cures, treatments, and even names for body parts are in my papyrus. I've also done a bit of surgery myself, and naturally I am very good at it.

Q: *Naturally. Tell us about your work as an architect.*

A: As you know, all pharaohs need a palace for their afterlives. I wanted to design something for Pharaoh Djoser that would really knock his sandals off. Anyway, I told him the old mastabas are much too small for a great king like him. I suggested we build a series of mastabas, each one slightly smaller that the one before, and stack them up. The whole thing would be like a giant stairway to heaven.

Q: *Dude, that rocks!*

A: Yes. It's made of stone, not that cheap and common mud-brick stuff, so it will last forever. They call it a step pyramid, you know. I think it's an absolutely brilliant piece of architecture.

Q: *Well, Imhotep, we can't thank you enough for chatting with us. The pyramid is pretty awesome, dude. What a brilliant idea!*

A: Glad you got the point.

Stepping up

Imhotep's step pyramid is all the rage with the royals—every pharaoh wants one. But as soon as the last stone is put in place, someone, somewhere is dreaming up a better pyramid. This someone is Pharaoh Sneferu, who rules around 2600 B.C. He knows he can build a pyramid that will leave Imhotep's effort in the dust. His son Khufu watches with interest. Will he be a chip off the old pyramid?

Imhotep's pyramid has six steps, so Sneferu takes the next logical...er, step. If he wants to go one better than that dude, he needs to add one more level. He constructs a seven-step pyramid. Somehow it's just not as big and monumental as he expects it to be. He tears up his plans and has a bit of a rethink. Back to the old drawing board!

Sneferu wonders if adding another level will make his pyramid look cooler. He tops off his pyramid with an eighth step. It's better, but it's still not quite there yet.

Then, the dude has a total brainwave. He decides to cover the step pyramid with smooth, straight sides. This outer casing will make the tomb difficult to access. But the super-cool thing is, it will give the pyramid the look of a ray of sunlight. Step pyramids may help a pharoah climb to heaven, but this awesome design will let you climb right up to the sun! Dude, it just doesn't get better than that.

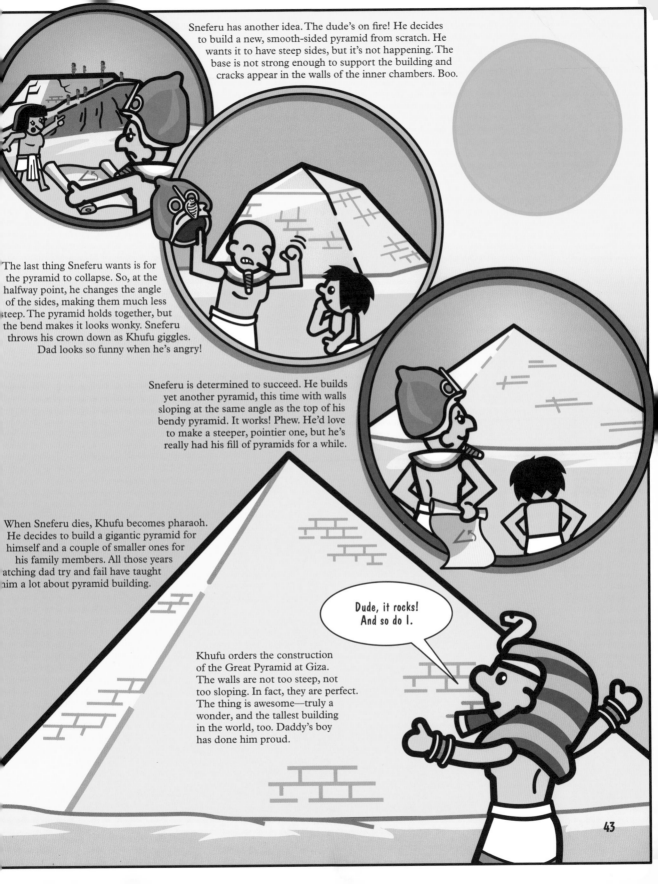

Sneferu has another idea. The dude's on fire! He decides to build a new, smooth-sided pyramid from scratch. He wants it to have steep sides, but it's not happening. The base is not strong enough to support the building and cracks appear in the walls of the inner chambers. Boo.

The last thing Sneferu wants is for the pyramid to collapse. So, at the halfway point, he changes the angle of the sides, making them much less steep. The pyramid holds together, but the bend makes it looks wonky. Sneferu throws his crown down as Khufu giggles. Dad looks so funny when he's angry!

Sneferu is determined to succeed. He builds yet another pyramid, this time with walls sloping at the same angle as the top of his bendy pyramid. It works! Phew. He'd love to make a steeper, pointier one, but he's really had his fill of pyramids for a while.

When Sneferu dies, Khufu becomes pharaoh. He decides to build a gigantic pyramid for himself and a couple of smaller ones for his family members. All those years watching dad try and fail have taught him a lot about pyramid building.

Dude, it rocks! And so do I.

Khufu orders the construction of the Great Pyramid at Giza. The walls are not too steep, not too sloping. In fact, they are perfect. The thing is awesome—truly a wonder, and the tallest building in the world, too. Daddy's boy has done him proud.

Construction crews

To build a massive structure, you need a massive workforce. Dude, we're talking a cast of thousands. There are the primary laborers who dig the quarry, haul the stone, and do masonry work. Lots of supporting dudes build ramps, keep the tools in working order, and mix up mortar. Let's catch up with Nebi, a stone hauler, and Rami, a quarryman, and find out what it's like to work on one of the biggest construction projects ever—a great big pyramid at Giza.

Q: *Hey dudes. Thanks for stopping to have a chat.*

A: (Nebi) Are you kidding? Thank you for giving me an excuse. My back is absolutely killing me. We'll have to be quick. We're on a break, but the overseer will make sure we don't stay away for too long. He's the ultimate slave-driver.

A: (Rami) My boss is just the same. What a jerk. They say this baby will take 20 years to finish. That's why I don't think 15 minutes here or there is going to make any difference.

Q: *So tell us about your work here. It all looks really exciting. All the dudes in Eygpt are talking about this amazing new project.*

A: (Nebi) Exciting? I think not. I drag big blocks of stone up and down the ramps all day. Woo hoo.

A: (Rami) Well, at least you get out and about. I'm stuck in front of a wall of stone all day. Chisel, chisel, chisel, plop. Chisel, chisel, chisel, plop. My mind goes numb just thinking about it. The same old rock face, day in and day out. Dullsville, dude.

Fancy a beer tonight, Nebi?

Sorry, Rami. The mother-in-law's aroun[d]

Payment at the pyramid

There is no money in Egypt, so in return for their work, laborers are given loaves of bread, jugs of beer, pieces of cloth, and other basics. Each family uses what they need and then swaps what is left with other families living near the pyramid.

Supervisors and high-status dudes get hundreds of loaves and lots of beer every day.

The standard ration for a working dude is ten loaves and a measure of beer.

Temporary workers are at the back of the line for the credits. It really sucks, dude.

Q: *I have to ask, why are you here if the work so boring?*

A: (Nebi) It's a job, isn't it? The work stinks, but the benefits aren't bad. There are about 5,000 of us who work here for a regular salary. We work together in gangs, with cool nicknames like The Drunkards of Mankaura. The guys like a giggle and a bit of friendly competition with the other gangs of workers—you know, to see who can load the most stones in the shortest amount of time. The dudes in charge have built a complete city for us to live in. Our wives and kids are here, too. I think it's cool that they've laid this on for us.

Q: *You say the benefits are good. Can you tell us a little more about how you are treated?*

A: (Rami) I can't complain about the food. There's loads of it. Of course, when you do a tough job like this one you have to keep your energy up, but they do lay on a spread. We even have beef...delish!

A: (Nebi) I appreciate the health care. I've seen guys break arms, get their legs caught between stones, you name it. If someone has an accident at work, the bigwigs make sure you get to a doctor right away.

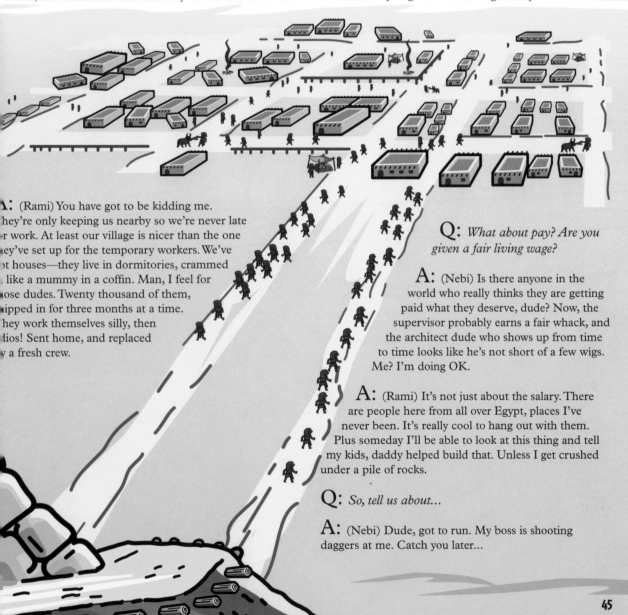

A: (Rami) You have got to be kidding me. They're only keeping us nearby so we're never late for work. At least our village is nicer than the one they've set up for the temporary workers. We've got houses—they live in dormitories, crammed in like a mummy in a coffin. Man, I feel for those dudes. Twenty thousand of them, shipped in for three months at a time. They work themselves silly, then adios! Sent home, and replaced by a fresh crew.

Q: *What about pay? Are you given a fair living wage?*

A: (Nebi) Is there anyone in the world who really thinks they are getting paid what they deserve, dude? Now, the supervisor probably earns a fair whack, and the architect dude who shows up from time to time looks like he's not short of a few wigs. Me? I'm doing OK.

A: (Rami) It's not just about the salary. There are people here from all over Egypt, places I've never been. It's really cool to hang out with them. Plus someday I'll be able to look at this thing and tell my kids, daddy helped build that. Unless I get crushed under a pile of rocks.

Q: *So, tell us about...*

A: (Nebi) Dude, got to run. My boss is shooting daggers at me. Catch you later...

45

Tomb raiders

They cross the desert sands to the pyramid, with only the moonlight to guide them. Its silvery beams glint off the copper chisels clutched in their hands. What are they doing out there in the dead of night? Even the donkey looks suspicious. They are a nasty gang of thieves, intent on robbing the tomb of its treasures.

The gang plots the robbery for a long time. The ringleader remembers his father telling him about the pyramid's secret passageways. (Often tomb robbers are the dudes who actually built them in the first place.) Even with this information, it will take a long time to get into the tomb, but they are determined. They fill baskets with mallets, chisels, food, and drink, load them onto their donkeys and sneak off into the night.

After many long nights, they reach a solid wall of tough granite rock. Those cunning pyramid builders have blocked off the corridor to the tombs! What a bummer. They work their way around the granite through the softer sides. It takes ages.

Under cover of darkness, they begin cutting a hole in the side of the pyramid. The donkey catches up on some sleep. At dawn, they must stop. Punishment for tomb robbers is harsh, and they cannot risk being seen. They chuck some sand over their work to disguise it and go home.

Sphinx on the up

Within roaring distance of the pyramids at Giza is the biggest, coolest cat: a gigantic statue known as the Great Sphinx. With the body of a lion and the face of a man, this big, bad kitty is an enormous 187 ft (57 m) long, 20 ft (6 m) wide, and 65 ft (20 m) tall. Pharaoh Khafre is building the statue to stand guard in front of his pyramid. They say he's even carving its face to match his own—and I'm not lion.

Roar materials

This mega-colossal catlike creature is carved from the limestone bedrock (that's the super solid rock that lies under the sands and surface rocks). Over time, diligent worker dudes shape the huge feline form, from the tips of its gigantic paws to a curled tail on its backside.

Topping it off

Lions represent royal power as well as strength, so what better way for a pharaoh to announce himself as top cat than by carving his own image into the stone? The *nemes* (headcloth) and ceremonial beard are just like the ones royals wear. A few coats of brightly colored paint, and this lion is ready to roar.

Well, that came out of the blue.

Hmm, wonder who's footing the bill for this?

Look, mate, it will be finished on Tuesday. You can carve it in stone.

Oww...would you keep your mallet off my mullet?

1425 B.C.

Sphinx can only get better

For a time, the shifting desert sands swallow the Great Sphinx, like cat poo buried in a gigantic litter box. Well, not really, but you get the idea. It is 1425 B.C., and the young prince Tuthmosis, out hunting in Giza, decides to have a little lie-down where the Sphinx is buried, which is up to its neck in sand. He takes a pause near the paws and has a pretty crazy dream.

Tuthmosis's dream

In his dream, the Great Sphinx speaks. It tells Tuthmosis that if he gets rid of all the sand, his reward will be the throne of Egypt. Tuthmosis's dudes start digging, eventually revealing the still-magnificent statue.

It's a stele

Tuthmosis becomes pharaoh, and decides to carve a special stone storyboard called a *stele* to share his amazing tale with the world. He puts it right in between the big cat's paws for everyone to check out.

So what's the deal?

Mysteries seem to swirl around the Great Sphinx like so much sand in the desert. Some people think the head of the Sphinx looks more like Khafre's brother. There are also those who think the face is the spitting image of Khafre's father. Other people argue about exactly how old it is. Whatever, dude...we can all agree that the awesome statue is the cat's meow.

I can dig it, dudes!

Oooh my back.

I need a beer break.

Oof, this thing is heavy. Couldn't he just send a thank-you card?

I needed a pit stop.

49

Into battle

It may be hot, but Egypt is a chilled place. There is an army, but it's a laid-back group, mostly used to sort out local troubles. Plus, the deserts surrounding the Nile are hard to cross, keeping out potential invaders. Then the Hyksos—a tribe from Asia—invades and the Egyptians have a rethink. They need an organized, well-trained fighting force, and better weapons. Before long, Egypt has a rocking, raiding army, supported by a shipshape navy. Bring it on, dude!

Fighting back

The Egyptians learn how to fight like the Hyksos, then use their newfound skills to overpower the invaders and chuck them out. They stop thinking defense and start thinking offense, so they leave Egypt to conquer an empire in Asia.

Charge!

Sometimes the pharaoh leads the attack, riding a horse-drawn chariot and wearing his special war crown. The most skilled warriors fight at the front, while newer recruits take up the rear. They sling rocks at the enemy—not exactly deadly, but very distracting. A well-aimed spear helps a warrior make his point. For up-close carnage, an axe is an excellent tool.

Bows and blades

The Hyksos invaders bring the *scimitar* (a curved-bladed sword) to Egypt and soon these lethal weapons are swinging everywhere. The Egyptians also nick their idea of using chariots for bow-and-arrow attacks. Archers can shoot their arrows in any direction as the chariot carries them into the heart of the battle. When they run out of arrows, there are spears on board to continue the assault. This army includes a group of African archers from Nubia—captives from an earlier raid, now fighting for the pharaoh.

Armed and dangerous

Seth (the Heroic Archers) division

Amun (the Mighty Archers) division

Re (the Many-Armed) division

This army is made up of three divisions named after Egyptian gods: Seth, Amun, and Re.

4,000 infantrymen (foot soldiers) in each division

1,000 chariot warriors in each division

The divisions are split into battalions of about 500 soldiers, and battalions are divided into companies of 250 men. At the top of the heap is the pharaoh, head dude in the army. A commander (often his son) reports to the pharaoh, and senior officers advise him.

Trade

The Egyptians can't complain. There's plenty of grain to eat and beer to drink. Rocks and mud along the Nile are used to build houses and temples, plus there's flax and hemp to weave into cloth. But what about the extras? Egyptians trade what they have for the stuff they don't. Traders load their donkeys or boats with Egyptian goods and travel to other lands to trade for raw materials and exotic goods. Trading is tricky, and bust-ups can occur with the locals, so the pharaoh oversees things to keep traders safe.

Mediterranean treats

Ships are a cheap and fast way to get cargo from A to B. Hot spots for Egyptian trade ships to swap goods are the countries bordering the Mediterranean Sea. They are practically next door. Pick up olive oil and wine in the Greek Islands, head to Cyprus for copper, or try timber on the eastern shores. Whatever floats your boat—it's out there.

Desert delights

There's more to the desert than sand, you know. In the eastern deserts along the Red Sea, dudes mine gold and emeralds. There are copper and turquoise mines here too, churning out the valuables. In the far western deserts, traders barter with the locals for goods such as salt from the Siwa oasis. The whole desert is like an enormous swap shop.

African bounty

Intrepid traders follow an ancient trade route right into the heart of Africa. They make the journey overland, helped by donkeys, loaded up with goods to trade. The donkeys move in a long line, kind of like a donkey traffic jam. This is a very tough route to travel and if there is any trouble, help can seem a long way off. But the rewards—ebony, ivory, and exotic animals—make the journey worthwhile.

Weights and scales

No money changes hands when Egyptians trade—they don't use it. Instead, people trade goods that they feel are of equal value. For example, they might trade two rolls of papyrus paper for a bag of dates. Done deal. Or, an item is given a price counted up in *debens*, which are a measurement of weight in copper or gold. Say, one baboon is worth 10 *debens*, and a giraffe is 30, you could trade a baboon for one-third of a giraffe. Sort of.

KEY

Olive oil
Squished to make oil, for burning in lamps

Leopard skins
Some priests wear skins around their shoulders

Ivory
Elephant tusks make combs, vases, and more

Giraffe skins
Covers furniture, while tail hairs are woven into cloth

Wine
Egyptians make beer and grow vines for wine

Incense
Smelly stuff for temples and tombs

Papyrus
Makes paper, which gets its name from papyrus

Wheat
A key ingredient in lots of tasty dishes

Gold
For glitzy statues and jewelry

Cattle
The horned type is particularly popular

Cedar wood
Great for building boats, furniture, and houses

Baboons
Popular pets in temples or palaces

Copper
Great for weapons and household goods

Ostrich feather
Makes brilliant fans and cool headdresses

Nile

This river is awesomely important for farming, and it's a big deal to traders, too. Trading fleets and small boats travel up and down the river. There are ports for loading goods that have been carried overland onto boats bound for the heart of Egypt.

Nubia

With its gold and copper mines, and access to the interior of Africa, this place is very interesting to Egyptians. The dudes have set up forts here, so they can keep watch on things (especially the gold).

Punt

For one-stop luxury shopping, you can't beat Punt. Myrrh trees to create the most divine incense for scenting the temple? Check. The finest elephant ivory and the most beautiful ebony? In stock. How about a baboon to liven up the place? No problem. Punt is the business.

Hatshepsut

This powerful dudette rules Egypt for 15 years, building trade with other nations and ordering the construction of super monuments. She's said to be a great beauty—although you wouldn't think so from her beard. Yes, beard. Hatshepsut runs the kingdom dressed as a dude. Find out why in this tale of cross-dressing and double-crossing.

Born to royalty in the 15th century B.C., Hatshepsut is daughter of Pharaoh Tuthmosis I and Queen Ahmose. No one wants a female pharaoh, so her parents marry her off to a half-brother whose mother is a commoner. When the pharaoh dies, this dude, also named Tuthmosis, becomes ruler.

Tuthmosis takes the name of Tuthmosis II (the sequel) and Hatshepsut calls herself "The Great Royal Wife." Whatever. She sticks her oar in a lot, telling her husband what to do. Maybe she thinks she can do a better job because she is 100 percent royal. Tuthmosis II only rules for a few years, and he has no children with Hatshepsut. He does have a young son whose mother is a commoner, though. Sound familiar?

When Tuthmosis II dies, little Tuthmosis III (the trilogy) is in line for the throne. But the brat's too young for the job, and Hatshepsut happily steps in. She rules as regent—the name for a dude who takes over when the real ruler can't rule, for some

After running Egypt as regent for several years, Hatshepsut decides she wants the top job for herself. The problem is, everyone wants a dude. So, she dons the royal crown, headdress, and false beard traditionally worn by the pharaoh. She gives her biography a spin, saying that her (very popular) dad wanted her to be pharaoh, and even claims to be daughter of the main god. Oh please.

This fake-out pharaoh becomes very powerful. She sends explorers to the land of Punt to bring back ivory, gold, and animals. She orders her temple to be built near the Valley of the *Kings*— dude, how messed up is that? If anyone finds it unusual that the pharaoh is a cross-dresser, no one says a word.

By now, Tuthmosis III is old enough to take action. He is bitter as sour grapes, and wants his crown back—fast! What happens next is a little fuzzy, but somehow Tuthmosis III gets rid of Hatshepsut. Maybe she dies of natural causes. Maybe the causes are not at all natural, if you know what I mean.

After her death, Tuthmosis III does all he can to erase Hatshepsut's name from history. All over Egypt, stonemasons chisel her name out and replace it with his. Her mummy is stolen and the tomb smashed to smithereens. Other monuments she had built are wrecked. The dude needs some classes in anger management.

I wear the pants in this family.

Akhenaten

Lots of dudes like catching rays on a sunny day, but Pharaoh Akhenaten takes sun worshipping literally. He turns his back on the Egyptian gods and says there is only one true god—the sun god Aten— and only Akhenaten can talk to him. Has this dude spent way too long in the sun?

Sunny side up

Amenhotep IV (same dude, different name) lives with wife Nefertiti in Thebes, the capital. Religion is a big deal here. There are thousands of priests who are loyal to the main god, Amun. Soon after Amenhotep becomes pharaoh, he starts messing around with the religion.

Tanfastic temple

Akhenaten tries to stop dudes from worshipping any other gods, insisting that Aten is the only god. He orders the construction of a brand-new capital city at Amarna. The place is awesome, with an open-air temple and a palace. Dudes can worship outside for the first time. They worship the god himself, instead of a statue—another first. In the art world, dudes had been made to look like gods, but Akhenaten thinks ordinary dudes should look just as they are. Great news for his beautiful wife, but a little harsh on his own droopy face and big bum.

He tells the priests that Aten (the sun) is the new god, and calls himself Akhenaten (servant of Aten). The priests are not happy, especially when he shuts the temples.

Religious wipe out

Every day is sun-day for Akhenaten and Nefertiti. They place offerings on the tables that lead to the altar and hold lavish religious ceremonies. But it's not all sunshine. Akhenaten is determined to wipe out the worship of other gods, especially Amun. He orders neighboring temples to be destroyed. Many dudes are angry that Akhenaten is hijacking their religion—but like this duck, they keep their beaks shut.

Smash and grab

After 18 years of rule, Akhenaten dies. Tired of worshipping the sun, the Egyptians are over the moon. They leave Amarna, wrecking the temples and defacing the images of Akhenaten, big bottom and all. Akhenaten's mummy disappears. The dude's history.

Treasure tomb

The Valley of the Kings is the final resting place for many great pharaohs, but inside the tomb chamber of Tutankhamun, no one's getting any rest. The funeral is over, the pharaoh's mummy is on the way, and just look at the place! The tomb workers are frantically trying to get everything ready, but they are running out of space, time, and patience. The tiny rooms are so cramped, the dudes keep knocking into each other, which doesn't help matters. Will they finish in this life or the afterlife?

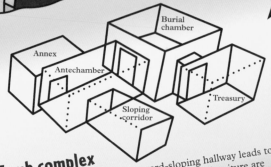

Tomb complex

Behind a doorway, a long, downward-sloping hallway leads to an antechamber (outer room) where beds and furniture are kept. From this room, one door opens to Tutankhamun's burial chamber and another to an annex storeroom for food and wine. Beyond the tomb is the treasury where Tutankhamun's canopic jars, containing his vital organs, rest.

Cram it in!

The scribe in charge of taking an inventory of the tomb's contents is very worried. How in the world are the workers going to stuff more than 5,000 things into such a small space? Trumpets, oars, boomerangs, ostrich feathers, board games, locks of his granny's hair, dog collars…the list goes on and on.

Super service

More than 200 shabti figures are locked away in the tomb. These are statues that represent the servants who will work for Tut in the next life.

Fine feast

The dead pharaoh will need to eat in the afterlife. More than 100 baskets and boxes of food and 30 jars of wine are placed in the tomb. The baskets are filled to the brim with things like bread, meat, honey, dates, and dried grapes. Yum!

illed to bursting

The tomb is crammed with furnishings: six beds,
a royal throne, three animal-shaped couches
glinting with gold, footstools, and chairs. There
is so much furniture the workers start stacking it.
They will have to take the six chariots to bits if
they are ever going to fit them in the same room.

Dress to impress

Tutankhamun will never run out of clean
loincloths. There are stacks of them, as well as
sandals, shawls, and aprons. Pots of cosmetics,
scented oils, and ointments are tucked away,
along with a mirror and razor so Tut can stay
stubble-free in the next life. For a bit of sparkle,
there are more than 200 pieces of jewelry.

Mummy
and mask

Third coffin

Second
coffin

First
coffin

Sarcophagus

Fourth
shrine

Third
shrine

Second
shrine

First
shrine

Boxed in

Tut's mummy and golden mask
rest inside three coffins, each one
slightly bigger than the one before
it. These are placed inside a
sarcophagus—a beautiful lidded
box carved from quartz stone. Four
shrines, each one a bit bigger than
the one underneath, enclose the
sarcophagus. The dude is totally
wrapped up safe and sound.

Ready for trouble

A full arsenal of bows, arrows, armor, and
shields is buried along with the pharaoh so
he can defend himself in the afterlife.

Stunning statues

There are loads of statues in the tomb. Some
are life-size in Tut's own image and decorated
with the finest gold, while others are in the
shape of animals.

Rameses the Great

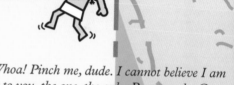

He rules his people for a whopping 66 years. He wins an incredible battle and signs the world's first official peace treaty. He builds spectacular temples, adorned with stone statues carved in his totally pharaoh-rific image. Somehow, he even finds time to father up to 100 children. Meet Rameses II, one of the most famous pharaohs in all of Egypt. But is he really all that, or is he merely bigging himself up to win a prime place in Egypt's history?

Q: *Whoa! Pinch me, dude. I cannot believe I am talking to you, the one, the only, Rameses the Great. I am not worthy.*

A: Of course you are worthy, young friend. Look, there's no need to bow down like that. Although it is rather fitting. OK, you can bow down for a little bit, and then we can begin. (Pause.) That will do nicely.

Q: *I just don't know where to start. You've had so many career highlights. I guess for me, the biggie is the battle with the Hittites at Kadesh. Talk me through it, dude.*

A: Very well, my child (and you might be—I have dozens of the blighters). Anyway, the Hittites are intent on expanding their empire. It's giving me the willies, frankly. I set off to try and capture the city of Kadesh, a place very loyal to the Hittites. I don't want to attract too much attention, so I show up with just my bodyguard and one small army division. The devious dudes in Kadesh tell me the army is a long way away. Because I am a really nice guy, I believe them. Liars! The army is just around the corner. It is a setup! As soon as we make our camp, we are attacked.

Q: *Crumbs! What happens next?*

A: I am afraid to say, many of my men panic and run away. Any fool can see that we are completely outnumbered. But Rameses the Great is made of sterner stuff. I get in my chariot and slowly but surely wipe those Hittites out. Victory will be mine!

Q: *Hang on a second. You fight an entire army all by yourself? That's kind of not what I heard. They say a backup army arrived right at the last minute to save your bacon, and when you got back to Egypt you put some spin on the story to make it look like you did it all by yourself.*

A: DO YOU DOUBT THE GREATNESS OF RAMESES THE GREAT?

Q: *Oh, no, no, no. I must have the story mixed up. Everyone agrees that you eventually make a peace treaty with the Hittites, the oldest surviving treaty of its kind. Cool. Then I guess you get back to your building work?*

A: Why, yes, that's true. I put up a rather fab fortress down in the western frontier. You know it, yes? But I must say my crowning achievement is the pair of temples at Abu Simbel, down in southern Egypt.

Q: *I haven't been there myself, but I've heard just the nicest things about it. Especially the statues!*

A: They are pretty amazing, you know. You must make a detour next time you are in the area. They celebrate my stunning victory at Kadesh. Both the temples are carved right out of the mountainside. There are four giant statues of me at the front— 65 ft (20 m) tall. You can't miss them, really. Quite a good likeness, I must say.

Q: *And what's inside?*

A: There are some small statues of the gods—it is a temple after all. And loads more statues of me, of course. You can never have too many!

Timeline

Don't know your Old Kingdom from your New Kingdom? Can't spot the difference between the Hittites and the Hyksos? Not quite au fait with your pharaohs? (It doesn't help that 11 of the dudes are called Rameses, now does it?) Don't be in de Nile: you need to put all the crazy Ancient Egyptians you've met in this book into context. Here's a timeline to show you who did what, when.

3100–2950 B.C.

The kingdoms of Upper and Lower Egypt unite and the era known as the Old Kingdom begins. Pharaohs are buried in mastaba tombs. The earliest known hieroglyphic writing appears—the first spelling mistake follows.

1539–1075 B.C.

Freaky pharaoh alert! Hatshepsut, the dudette who dresses as a dude, rules. Akhenaten tries to make everyone worship the sun. Tutankhamun goes to the afterlife with excess baggage.

1539–1075 B.C.

Ahmose decides enough is enough. He drives out the Hyksos and unites Egypt. Kings are buried in fantastically lavish tombs cut into cliff walls and valley floors in the Valley of the Kings.

1075–715 B.C.

Looking unsettled, dude. Royal power ain't what it used to be, and Egypt's grip on the region loosens. A Nubian king conquers Egypt. The Nubians want to sort the place out, and bring back some of the cool stuff about Egypt's culture.

715–404 B.C.

It seems like everyone wants a crack at ruling Egypt, dude. The Assyrians invade for a while, then Egypt is conquered by the Persians. Will Egypt ever be independent again? Yes indeed, dude...but not for long.

2950–2575 B.C.

A capital for the newly united Egypt is built at Memphis on the Nile. Imhotep, chief architect for Pharaoh Djoser, stacks mastabas on top of each other, each one smaller than the last, to build a step pyramid. Who can top this?

2575–2150 B.C.

Pharaoh Khufu tops it! His Great Pyramid of Giza rises from the desert, guarded by the enormous Sphinx. Hello kitty! Workers take 20 years to build it.

630–1520 B.C.

thundering chariots! The Hyksos
vaders, warriors from Asia, roll into
orthern Egypt. They grab the north,
hile the pharaohs rule the south
om Thebes.

1975–1640 B.C.

Hooray! The ruler of Thebes, Mentuhotep, reunites Egypt. His reign marks the start of the New Kingdom. Under Senworsret I and III, Egypt invades Nubia, its trading partner for goodies south of Egypt.

2125–1975 B.C.

Egypt hits a rough patch. Dudes argue over who is in charge. Pretty soon, it's splitsville for Egypt. Egypt is divided again into two smaller states, ruled from Memphis in the north and Thebes in the south.

332–305 B.C.

The Macedonian king Alexander the Great conquers Egypt, and founds a new capital at Alexandria. Wonder how he thought up that name! His general, Ptolemy, becomes pharaoh.

332–30 B.C.

The super-cool Rosetta Stone is carved—it rocks. Cleopatra becomes ruler of Egypt. A Roman dude then conquers Egypt, which becomes part of the Roman Empire. End of an era and all that…

INDEX

ACKNOWLEDGMENTS

Rich Cando dedicates this book to the following dudes:

Friends, family and fans for supporting the expansion of the "Dude" universe, and specifically Richard and JoAnn Cando for making my personal history possible.

Laura Buller dedicates this book to:
Alice (you rule) and Sean (you rock)

Dorling Kindersley would like to thank:
Constance Novis for proofreading.

The illustrator would like to thank:
Assistant Illustrators: Anthony Conley, Nicolette Davenport, Warren Lee, Zim McCurtis, James Morphew, Keith Tiernan, Steffen Vala

Assistant Sketch Artists: Erin Fusco, Mike Robinson, Misaki Sawada, Steffen Vala

Color Corrections: Melissa Bolosan, Rodney Collins, James Morphew, Leslie Saiz

Rich Cando's Representation: Hal Kant

The author would like to give big ups to all the young dudes at DK:
Julie Ferris, Jim Green, Andrea Mills, Diane Thistlethwaite, and Lin Esposito, and props to Peter Chrisp for keeping it real.

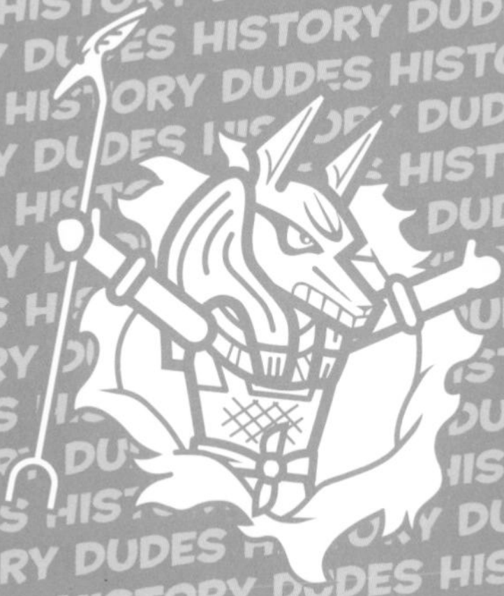